VOLUME V

Finding Balance

WRITTEN BY: MAKEDA GORDON

Copyright © 2016 by Nizaree West

All Rights Reserved. No parts of this book may be reproduced in any form without the express written consent of Publisher/Authors, except in the case of brief quotations embodied within relevant articles and book reviews for print ad electronic media.

TABLE OF CONTENTS

Preface ……………………………….... i

Introduction ……………………….…… ii

Grounding (The Origin) ………………1

Happiness Is a State of Being …………11

You Are Valuable   …………………25

Loving Completely   …………………36

Self-Expression   …………………...47

Honoring Your Intuition …………….58

We Are One   …………………..70

Epilogue …………..……………………78

Preface

Being a woman is a tough mantle to carry. We are required to do and be everything to everyone. Our families dictate how we should behave; Our children get to choose our daily schedules; Our Significant Other determines our emotional status, and our Careers tell us what we are worth. At what point do we get to simply "BE"?

Juggling so many balls at one time without a break, we are bound to drop one. Unfortunately, the ball that generally gets dropped is Us. However, that does not have to be the case, if we learn how to Balance our lives better. Finding that proper balance is not always easy, but now we have some practical tools that can be easily applied to bring us the peace that we so desperately seek.

Introduction

There are Seven Major Layers to a person. Identifying them and balancing them is the key to Love, Peace and Happiness.

In this read, we are going to Identify, Detoxify and Balance out those Layers. Not taking the time to bring yourself a since of grounding and purpose will eventually cause you to burn out. Which, in turn, makes us good to no one at all.

As a woman, we are the backbone to the family unit. We are the creators of the environment in which our families live. We are the first teachers and nurturers of the next generation. In essence, we are the Foundational Force to all things that will be. I know that sounds exhausting, but the truth is, there is no greater gift on earth than Woman. We are indeed Phenomenal Beings. It's all about Management!

How do we know what to Manage? Well, the first thing we must do is evaluate all the things that we are Managing right now.

Am I seeing the big picture clearly, or, have is my vison skewed? Have I made my life's decisions based on what I know to be right, or, what I have been taught is right? How do I know the difference? These are just a few questions that we need to address in an effort to finding that Balance needed for the most productive life.

In order to decipher between the two, we have to go to the Origin of our belief system. That means, going further back than what Mommy and Daddy may have taught you. It is actually looking at the Origin of the shift in Family and Feminine values. Realizing that, will reveal the "why" behind your particular upbringing, your mother's upbringing and so on.

"Finding Balance" is going to require some reprogramming of your current mind set and belief systems. Not necessarily because they were intentionally wrongly implanted, but, because they were strategically calculated by ones of no direct connection to you or your loved ones.

As quiet as it has been kept, there were and is a group of people who decided for us all how we should think, feel and operate in our daily lives. We were deliberately served an agenda to create and maintain a life of psychological, emotional, financial and environmental oppression. Removing the shackles that bind you is not an unattainable task, but, it is a task that will require diligence and persistence. If, you believe that you possess these attributes, redemption is Yours.

v

EMPRESS MAKEDA GORDON

THE

ORIGIN

EMPRESS MAKEDA GORDON

When we speak about the Origin of a thing, we are looking to find where it began. There is no effective way to understand the operating systems of women today without looking back to where our gender's mentality was reprogrammed. "Women's Liberation Movement", it was a powerful time in life for us. We became what we considered to be "independent, self-reliant, liberated, equal" and so on. We took a stand for ourselves. Knowing that we should be view as and allowed the same basic privileges as a man. Sounds about right, wouldn't you say; but how did Women's Lib truly affect the dynamic of the feminine lifestyle? What did it do to or for our psyche?

Well, we are definitely more Independent than ever, our wages are within a hairline of a man's; we are standing on our own two feet, with or without a husband; we are raising our children alone in most cases;

obtaining the same positions in the workforce as men; I guess you can say we won the battle. Or did we?

Prior to the Movement, the family structure was intact, as it pertains to the original order of things during creation. Husbands worked and provided for their family, raised and reared their children as well as covered and protected their homes. Wives took care of the household, served as the nurturer, or calming force if you will, to her family. They raised their children hands on and supported their husbands in whatever was needed. Most women were Business Owners, working from home to help with the needs of the family without sacrificing the home. The children minded their parents. They were respectful and hard working. This way of life can be considered the Ultimate Balance.

Fast forwarding to today, where are we now? The men are no longer in the home. Most children have no relationship or respect for their absentee fathers. As for the women, we have been "Promoted". We now get to work those jobs that we fought so hard to get, sometimes 50-55 hours a week; we get to continue to maintain the upkeep of our homes; let us not forget we are now the protectors of our domains as well; best of all the nurturing and calming nature of us is still a requirement whenever possible because most times our children are being raised by the systematic provisions or by each other. We have given the power over to society to rear our children into what they will have them to be. You have no control any longer. If your day starts at 7AM and you do not return home until 6-7pm, then there is dinner (for those who cook), "your" wind down time and maybe a few chuckles before bedtime, that gives you about 2 hours a day that you are parenting. On the other hand, your child's day consist of seven hours of school system, a two-hour afterschool program/activity, and let's not forget their friends and interest. All of these things are standing in the gap for teaching your children in place of you the parent. So I ask you again, how has Women's Liberation supported you personally and as a family unit?

Empress Makeda Gordon

Let us take a look at the alternative to the workforce. We have the welfare system. This system is the greatest of all oppression. In order to even receive any support, the man has to be absent from the home. Taking into account the little bread crumbs they provide you with, how does one live? If you do get a job to supplement your income they cut your "benefits" and if you don't you live well below the poverty level. They now require you to become a part of a work program and/or school to maintain this hand out, but, college is not an option, which would put you in a better position for a better job, because it is unaffordable. So you are forced into these trade programs that are saturated in the actual field of work. Why, because they are limited in industry and everyone is in them. This leaves you with a certification without work. Not to mention the low wages that come with these fields which put you back at square one in terms of provision. These conditions ultimately drain the energy from your personal motivation to get ahead because you can no longer see a way out. In which case, many women result to indecent behavior to make ends meet, while others resort to self-medicating through the means of drugs, alcohol and reckless lifestyles. At the end of the day, the ones being affected the most are the children. They are being trained by your life not your words. Very few are able to break out of the poverty box.

Now, if I may play devil's advocate for a moment; what is women's lib didn't exist? What would 2016 look like? Here's a theory.

If women were not as present in the workforce and it was dominated by men, because we make up half of the population, that would mean that there would be less money to share. What I mean by that is this, our husband's would possibly be paid more because there are fewer employees; which could also increase job security as well. This notion could greatly impact our individual households financially. We, the wives could continue with our legal hustles utilizing our talents as we used to. In turn, the children are rooted in a structured home receiving a wealth of character and life building lessons which would catapult them into successful lives as well. While this is a beautiful thought for me to ponder, we will never know if that would have been the outcome.

It is my belief that this re-programming of women was a strategic plan to divide and conquer the masses. How many wealthy families do you know that have single parent homes? There are very many middle class families in that position. It appears to be geared to keeping the poor poor and the rich rich; and that is not a racial issue, it is an issue of financial status. But, that is another topic for another day. The question is, where do we go from here, and how do we get back to the basics?

GROUNDING YOURSELF

How does One Ground Ones-Self? What does Grounding even mean? To be grounded means to be fully aware of who you are, how protected you are and how provided for you are. In other words, to be Grounded, means to Know that you are well and everything will be alright, in spite of what comes your way.

Yes, I know that may seem like a naive way to look at life, but it is a fact.

Nothing can be balanced unless the foundation is firm. We have taken a look inside of some of the reasons we may feel the overwhelming forces of life, now let's see how we can recreate a firm foundation on solid ground.

The process of building a strong foundation begins with digging up. We must dig deep enough to re-stabilize and refill with new concrete (thinking). Now believe me, I am not one who would advise that we all go back to being barefoot and pregnant, so to speak. That ship has sailed and the damage has been done. However, what I am suggesting is that we identify with the personal damages, cut away the "stinkin thinkin" and elevate.

WHAT GOES UP MUST COME DOWN

In order to elevate your mind to a higher level of thinking, you have to come down off of your high horse and realize that you are no more entitled or special than any of The Most High's creation. After all He said that "ALL Things Work Together…". Did you take that to mean only life experiences? If so, you missed the essence of that Scripture. ALL means ALL. There is not one living being on the face of this earth that is not intertwined in some way. We need nature as much as nature needs us. Accepting this truth will begin to transform your mentality.

The Most High not only created all things, but loves all creation and provides for all creation. That includes you.

Think about this for a moment….

It has also been written that "You reap what you sow…", is it your understanding that, that pertains to giving alone? What if I told you that every thought, action, motive, dollar, time, etc., were all seeds that we sow. If nature is in fact our resource for food, light, heat and so on, why is it that we do not see that how we interact with nature is our seeds for the future reaping. If you do not believe me just read up on the Ozone Layer for example.

Grounding yourself is literally becoming one with Creation. Respecting it and honoring the fact that God makes no mistakes; meaning everything serves a purpose. Now, that doesn't mean you have to start camping or anything. It simply means that you are doing your part for preservation of life. Acknowledging its usefulness.

You and I both know that all living beings outside of Humanity is provided naturally. How much more do you think that you will be provided for as God's Elect. Created in His image and given the brilliance of mind. The earth itself, is a provision for us. So if you realize that you surely must realize our need for it. He created all things that we would need prior to creating us. That means provision always comes first. If you can wrap your mind around that, half the battle is already won.

Empress Makeda Gordon

Happiness

Is

A State of Being

Empress Makeda Gordon

Happiness, the one thing we all have in common, the pursuit of it. We tend to search for it as if it is a tangible thing that we can possess. When in fact, Happiness is a belief system, a faith based thing, if you will. The scripture teaches us "As a man thinketh in his heart, so is he"; are you able to grasp the true meaning in that statement? Most of us believe that our prayers are answered because of our faith in God's ability to grant them. Others believe that if we set our minds to do a thing we will accomplish it. Bottom line here is we stand on what we believe in no matter what others may think or feel about our faith system. So my question to you is why is this mode of thinking not applicable to our happiness?

Happiness is a State of Being, that means that it just IS. It is not, or should not be predicated on what any outside force determines it to be, but, it should be our choice and our truth. Who or What is getting in the way of your Happiness?

The ability to embrace a Happy State of being is determined by a few different things. Those things include but are not limited to how you view your right to be Happy.

- ❖ Self Esteem
- ❖ Self-Worth
- ❖ The internalization of others misery
- ❖ Your commitment to being happy
- ❖ Your decision making
- ❖ The circle of people you surround yourself with.

Let's break these components down.

Self Esteem

The Comedian, Katt Williams, said it best. Your Self Esteem is how you feel about you. How can someone affect how you feel about you?

If you have read Layers Vol. One, you will have identified ways in which life experiences can impact your Self Esteem, however, once you have worked the process of healing, you learn that no one can have that much power over you that they dictate your life unless you give it to them. You have a choice to hold yourself responsible for another human being's short comings or not. It is imperative to remember that Every pot sits on its own bottom; in other words, every man is responsible for his own actions. It is their decision to misuse or abuse you, but, it is your decision to allow it.

Rebuilding or maintaining your self-esteem has very little to do with another person's actions and everything to do with your personal actions and how strongly you believe in them being right. A woman with a strong set of Morals and a defined Character, is a woman that is sure of herself.

Self-Worth

What is your perception of you, as a woman? What is it that you deem a "worthy" human being? Those questions are rhetorical. Answer them within.

Self-Worth begins with first Knowing, knowing who you are, what you believe and what you stand for. Without these basic understandings you can never truly realize your worth. Seeing yourself as worthy is easier said than done. It will take some chopping away at doctrine and social requirements.

The beginning is realizing one simple truth, you belong to the Most High and are created in His image and His likeness. Accepting this as you're beginning is a great start. The very clarity that when we are created, He chose us to take dominion of the earth, should allow you the understanding that you are special. He could have made any one of His creation ruler but He chose us. We procreate, nurture, and set order in this earth. We possess the power to speak things into existence. No other being outside of Himself is capable of that. Do you ever wonder why?

What does it truly mean to be created in "His Image"? In order to be able to fully get that statement, we must move from understanding to Overstanding. To Overstand a thing, you have moved past basic comprehension and have learned how to apply that which you understand to your practical living. Let's take a moment to break this thing down.

Genesis 1:27 "So God created man in his own image, in the image of God created he him; male and female created he them".

If I were to give what this scripture mean to me, I would pull out certain words that stick out for me. For instance, "Own"; when I read this verse, I see that I am created to look like God expected, to be all that He imagined me to be. Then, I look at "in the image of God created he him", to me, that is a solidification of My Image to the Most High, which would be as HE saw me to be. Sliding down to verse 28, He gave me all power over the earth "and take dominion over the fish of the sea, and over the fowl of the air, and over EVERY LIVING THING that moveth upon the earth". Wow! What an honor that is for Him to see me as worthy to possess such power.

When I think about these scriptures, I cannot help but to "overstand" my worth;

because if the Creator Himself saw and deemed me worthy, who am I to question His authority. So I stand tall and strong in the knowing that I was not born but created. My purpose is to take dominion. There is never a Ruler put in place that is not capable and/or worthy of the land trusted to him.

So to recap, My God sees me in His image, not in my vision, not in my ability, not in my flaws, but, in His image. What exactly is the Image of the Most High to you?

I see Him as being Omni. Omnipresent: present in all places at all times, Omniscient: having infinite awareness, understanding and insight; knowing all things, Omnipotent: Almighty or unlimited power: an agency or force of unlimited power and influence, Omnificent: creating all that comes into existence; unlimited in creative power. How do you see Him?

If I am right about Who He is, that would make me pretty significant in this world.

Internalization of Others misery

How often do you find yourself being a good friend/family member by listening to some one's hardships and ending up internalizing them before you realize it? Did you know that you can adopt some one's energy by simply allowing them to connect their problems with your heart? Some of you may be used to the phrase, "spirits attach themselves to you", well a spirit is simply an energy force. Why and how does this happen?

The truth is, not everyone is capable, right away, to be some ones support system. If you, yourself, are not fully healed and living on a higher level, you will cause yourself more injury by attempting to handle an issue you have not yet overcome. A prime example of this would be a drug addict. If you are still in your addiction, how do you see yourself walking into a drug house to tell someone else not to use? Realistically, you wouldn't. Nine times out of ten, you may speak to them and give them all the advice you can; you may even be able to empathize with how they became an addict and what keeps them addicted, but, since you, yourself are still in your addiction, you will exit that house with a little something for yourself. What I am saying is, if you've recently had a break up that you haven't gotten over, you cannot lead another woman into her healing. You must first be far removed from a thing to effectively be able to address it. Once you have walked the path of forgiveness, healing and letting go, you are not ready for every topic of discussion. The effects of doing this can be detrimental.

    Here is one more example. Have you ever gotten a phone call from your girlfriend and she is hysterical, she just found out that her boyfriend was cheating on her? Now, you may have experience this very same issue earlier on in your relationship, or maybe in a past relationship or two. If you are not healed from those wounds, her conversation will bring up all those feelings, now her problems have become yours, even though that is not a current problem you personally are facing. This conversation penetrates your subconscious and manifest through your actions more than your words. You become insecure in your relationship without just cause. This behavior may reveal itself by you doing things you've never done or never had to do before. Such as, over questioning, checking phones, tracking whereabouts, etc. In other cases, it may rear its head in your moods. Some women become agitated more easily, others may take an introverted approach, where they are creating scenarios in their own minds but not speaking out; and then you have your women who become out right confrontational. Whichever one path you take, it is not your battle, it is the heroin in you that made you believe that you could handle anything; but what cost are you paying to be the "good Samaritan".

Your Commitment to Happiness

How important is being happy, to you? Is happiness your true desire; or are you so accustom to being unhappy that you settle for that familiar feeling? There are times that we campaign for dysfunction and don't even realize it. So, how can you tell if you are truly for or against happiness?

The first indication is to evaluate your decision making skills. Do you make life decisions that move you closer or further from your goals? You can also take a close look at the people you spend the most time with, outside of your children. Not those who you care the most about, but those you spend your time with. You may ask why; the reason is because we tend to surround ourselves with two types of people, on a regular basis; the first type is those that are struggling a bit more than we are. Our reasoning for having these people around are not usually for us to mentor, but, to make us feel better about ourselves. The second type is usually the people who feed our negative emotions and co-sign our foolish behaviors. We keep these people near to justify not growing. Now, you may not even realize that this is your circle, but, if you are effectively evaluating, you will see how we make this mistake. Either way, neither type is supporting our desire to find what happiness truly is. In fact, they become a false manifestation of happiness because we are only happy for as long as they maintain the same behaviors that we need from them.

Your commitment to Happiness needs to be in spite of not because of outside interference.

Decision Making

The choices we make for our lives will directly affect your ability to maintain a happy state of mind. When we continuously make bad decisions for our lives, it is a ripple effect. Remember earlier when we spoke about reaping and sowing? This is another example of that. For instance, staying on a job where you are underpaid and overworked; staying in a relationship that you don't see a positive future in; consistently mismanaging your money and so on. These behaviors, when you know better, can eat away at your trust in yourself. They also will only give you as much of a return as they are capable of. Staying in a dead in job will only make you feel stuck with no way out; sitting in a relationship that has no future becomes harder and harder to exit the longer you are there, in turn time passes and the feelings of "what's the point" kicks in; and finally, consistently mismanaging your money by living above your means and/or not prioritizing your responsibilities will leave you in a pool of debt and with a poverty mentality. I believe you are getting the point.

Your Circle

      We have touched on the types of people that are closest to us, but this section is about your circle. Your circle consists of 4 basic areas of your life; Home, Work, Family, Friends. The difference between your closest people and your circle is that your closest people are chosen by you and your circle is most times not completely in your control. We tend to be adopted into some of these relationships. For instance, we don't get to choose our family members or who we have to interact with at work. These people have their purpose in your life. Glean what you can and leave what you don't need. Do not pick up their habits, characteristics or behaviors unless you see it as an attribute you want to possess. Otherwise, each time you are in their presence you will find your mood changing for the worst.

Empress Makeda Gordon

If you take anything away from this chapter, allow it to be the clear "Overstanding" that it is You and You alone responsible for your Happiness. People, places and things are only here to add to what already exist. Do not allow yourself to become the puppet to the many puppet masters in this world. Find your peace and Happiness through living a life that you can feel proud of in spite of the feedback from those around you. Once you find your happiness, stand in it and plant yourself. Let nothing or no one alter that for you.

Empress Makeda Gordon

You Are Valuable

Empress Makeda Gordon

Value: the regard that something is held to deserve; the importance, worth, or usefulness of something or someone.

Sometimes we have to go back to the basics on a word to understand it, not all the ways in which we have heard it used. People have a way of redefining things for us based on their perception. It is up to you to define all the words that describe you and everything pertaining to you. Remember words have power, so be careful what words you allow to be spoke to or over you.

If we were to go to the majorities belief in the moment of creation of man and woman, that thought gives us a beautiful ideal. To think that the Creator drew from the dirt and created man, but, that moment, He saw a need for woman…. The story says that he looked at Adam and said that it was not good for man to be alone, and that he would create for him a helpmeet. Just let that sink in for a moment. How wonderful woman must be.

When you think of the task that Adam had before him with the cultivating of the earth, God could have very well created him some physically strong help to lighten his burden. Now I know most of us women would like to think that the thought "it is not good for man to be alone" meant that Adam needed a woman for his physical needs; but if you think about it, there were no women. That means nothing to, let's say put a rise in his loins. So it was not about Adams sexual needs that called for woman to exist. (Ok, so this is indeed my perception, but if you give it some thought, you may actually see what I am speaking of) Just hear me out.

When God decided to create woman, He was thinking Creation. I presume it would have been much simpler to just draw us from the dirt as he did Adam; but He did not do that. He actually placed man into a coma, entered his body and pulled from him a vital part which was positioned to protect the most important organ man can possess. Why would he leave man in such a vulnerable state? Survival is possible without full usage of any organ in the body with the exception of the heart. So this was in fact, the first time God allowed man to be vulnerable to woman. Then He formulated woman from that rib, or, the protector of our life source if you will. In that process of molding our shell, He took His time and added some curves and such to distinguish man from woman. With Creation on His mind, He decided that it would be us from which all humanity would continue. Giving us a womb and building an entire system within us for reproductive purposes.

So you see ladies, sex was the benefit of reproduction, but never was it your sole purpose in this world. The moment we see ourselves "in His image" is the moment we overstand our Value. I know that society is doing a wonderful job at making us see ourselves as an object of a man's affection; but the truth is, We are man's life source. I say this to bring you into the fullness of understanding of who you are, not to in any way cause you to see yourself above men in anyway.

Woman is so absolutely strategically made that there is no deigning our Value. Just in case you are still unsure, let me reveal to you some ways that we have been trained to see things differently. I say trained because there was a point in time that we were clear that we are indeed Royals. But, over time we have been stripped so bare that all we have left is shame as our garment. What could have possibly brought our self-image so low? The answer is years and years of abuse and subliminal messaging.

If we were to take a look at what we have been taught about our history and the way our women were treated, you can't help but to feel some type of way. However, some of us have the ability to disassociate ourselves from our Ancestors; but what they cannot disassociate themselves with is the reality that we live in today and the vague memories we were exposed to early on, along with the stories from our parents and grandparents. The image is still the same, with the exception of the extreme violence in most cases.

Empress Makeda Gordon

Our biggest challenge today is the entertainment industry. This is where the subliminal messaging takes place. It has increasingly become unbearable over the years. My question is how is it that we do not see the damage that some artist is causing? There was a major out pour from parents over gangster rap music. Once they began to see our sons acting out the lyrics to these songs and getting themselves killed or in prison, we cried out loud. I have yet to see the same magnitude of out pour for the female artist that are creating an image of female sex symbols or the lyrics in their music that promotes promiscuity and/or the manipulation of men with the use of their bodies (that is a form of witchcraft).

The media has been training us to look, act and think a certain way for years, and generation after generation is compliant. So what do we need to do to break the cycle? Deprogramming and reprogramming is a start.

When we think about deprogramming, we have to begin at our beginning. This means figuring out if you are a product of the environment in which you were raised. Think about mom, grandma, auntie, cousins and any other significant female in your life. Did you see a high turnover of relationships, scandalous attire, cheaters, manipulators, gold diggers, etc., etc.? As we said earlier, in Chapter one, children learn more from watching than they do listening. What habits or character traits did you pick up, if any? In addition to those people, do not forget the friend choices you've made up to this point. Sometimes, even if we are not exhibiting a behavior, it doesn't mean the residue of it has not penetrated us in some way.

To reprogram means to program again. If you did see a lot of indecent behavior, that doesn't mean that you do not have a foundation of rightness. Remember what all went into creating you by The Most High. Remember He saw and sees you in His image. With that in mind, you have something great to build on. Take into account what His plan and purpose for your life is and you will begin to see the value in your existence.

A woman who Values herself, carries herself in a manner that commands certain treatment. It is identified in your dress, your walk, the words you choose to speak and the company you keep.

There was a time when what you wore was how exposed you for who you really were. Now a days that point is up for debate in the minds of most. Women have taken the stance that they can wear anything and should not be judged by their attire. This is just not true. In biblical times, if you were poor your clothing told on you; Righteous women dressed modestly, whores dressed for customers and clergy even had a specific attire. So when you see women today being disrespected on the street and becoming angered by it is absurd. We train people how to treat us without ever saying a word.

It was back in the day as it is today, husbands choose their wives by the level they are on. The wealthy rarely choose the poor as the distinguished rarely choose the wayward. You have to remember life today is a dress rehearsal for the part you want to play in the future. The question is, what role are you auditioning for, the Queen or the peasant?

The power that a woman possess is indeed between her legs, but, that power is the goddess in her, her ability to create. Never allow your authority to be traded in from ruler to the courts jester. That place is how life continues. It is where life begins. We were not given such a beautiful gift for the entertainment or abuse from anyone. When you, first, honor your own body, everyone else will follow.

It is possible that you have been living on a lower plane for some time now, but it is never too late to make a change. Those changes can be broken into three phases; the Mind, the Heart, and the Physical.

The Mind

You have to transform your thinking. The only way to do this is to educate yourself on your lineage. Most formal educational systems begin our history with slavery or some other great oppressive time. You have to ask yourself, who were we before all of that, then go on a quest for knowledge. Find out is all you know is all there is to know and how much of it is true. Once you see how beautiful your beginnings were, you will begin to see what lies beneath all of the Layers and the smoke screens you have been exposed to. It's like stepping out of the Matrix. Take that knowledge and own it because it is yours. Your family runs deeper than the generations you know.

The Heart

Scripture says "Out of the mouth flows the issues of the heart". That means, the attitudes, anger, negative words and defeatist jargon all come from a place deep in your heart. Cut away the pain and everything that comes with it; fill it with all of the love and blessings you can remember and still see. If you are mindful of how truly blessed you are and where you could or should be based on decisions you made as well as those made for you to this point, that alone will show you how much your Maker values you. In turn, you will begin to only speak words of love and kindness to others and to yourself, which will be a planting of new seeds that will yield a wonderful harvest.

The Physical

Once you have adjusted your thinking concerning yourself and become more loving and secure, it will change how you present yourself. You won't feel the need to require or accept just any kind of attention you can get. Those skin tight dresses and tiny little shorts will become uncomfortable for you. You won't be concerned with throwing your hips a little harder when walking by men, because you will know that a man who deserves you will be looking for something deeper, and so will you. A woman's true beauty is in her elegance. Will the real Ladies please stand?!?

Empress Makeda Gordon

LOVING COMPLETELY

There are four basic types of love, **Eros, Phileo, Storge and Agape**. In order to Love Completely, we need to explore each type individually. Once we have a clear picture of what love is in its proper perspective, we can then operate in it effectively.

<u>Phileo Love</u>

Phileo is the Greek word for affection. This type of love is the most general of them all. It applies to a wide spectrum. The love you have for humanity, your friends and associates, pets and so on. This Love level is generally related to a Soul Love. During creation the scripture states that God blew the breath of life into us and we became a living Soul. That is what the Greek referred to Phileo as a Soul Love; the average human being, until taught otherwise, is born with a natural affection for people as a whole. This love is effortless and often times unwarranted.

Having the ability to have love in your heart for all creation is a wonderful gift to possess. I am sure you would agree that in a perfect world we would have stayed that way and life as we know it would be much different.

Because this love is a natural as the air we breathe, it is the most vulnerable of them all. It can easily be altered by life's experiences and the teaching of those around us. We must get back to Phileo Love if we want to see a change in how we interact with each other on a wider scale.

This is the love that the good book speaks of when we are told to Love our brother as we do ourselves. That is a mandate from the Most High and He does not give a law, precept, or commandment without it yielding some benefit to our lives.

If you gave some real thought to your level of Phileo Love, you may be able to determine whether you are receiving your fair portion and why.

To simplify this love type, it is basically how you interact with and treat people as well as creation. For example, if you are consistently losing "friends" you may want to ask yourself if you are showing yourself friendly. Are you finding that you are unable to get along with coworkers, no matter where you work, if so, that is a sign to check your Phileo Love layer.

It is true when that say you get back everything you put out into the universe. Having a heart of love and kindness will return love and kindness to you. Most people don't believe that. Have you ever heard anyone say "good guys finish last"? Well I believe that to be a myth. I know that there are many experiences out there to say I am wrong, but let me share my perspective.

First, allow me to clarify that operating in Phileo Love does not mean you have to be foolish or vulnerable. We always need to use discernment with whom we allow into our inner circle. With that being said, dealing in this soulish realm of love, in most cases, these people are not family. Therefore, you are the one that makes the ultimate choice who you let get that close to you. We are capable of loving folks from a distance. There will always be a couple that fool us and slip through the cracks, but to say "always finish last", says that you are making some bad choices repeatedly.

Storge Love

The word Storge refers to Family Loyalty; so this realm of love applies to your relatives. Again, an area that we naturally gravitate to. We don't get to choose our family members and most time we just automatically love them simply because they are family.

Now the importance of this particular type of love is it's training abilities for us. As they say, our cousins are our first best friends, we learn what love is and how it should feel through our interaction with our family members. The problem is, that experience is not always a good one and can hurt us more than help us. If we don't have a positive experience with love as a child it is almost impossible to maintain the Phileo Love that you were born with.

Our family relationships have shaped most of us into who we are today. Watching parental love as it pertains to you taught you to love or dislike yourself; parental love amongst themselves taught you what romantic love should be; interaction with your grandparents showed you love and respect for your elders, and so on and so on. This realm of love is the most dangerous. Why? Because blood is involved. Where ever blood is, the effects run deep.

So what if you didn't have the healthiest examples of love within your family, have you taken the time to see how or if it is affecting your relationships outside of the family? Sometimes there are open wounds that need to be healed in order to elevate. We walk through that process is Layers Volume One: Who Am I? Why Am I?

Eros Love

Eros Love is the one we all long for, Romantic love. It has to do with intimacy and sexual relations. We long for this level so much that we find ourselves creating it where it doesn't exist.

This particular Love type can be the most damaging long term. The fact that it includes sex is what makes it that. Sex and intimacy are the things that we don't, or aren't supposed to share abroad. However, we seem to and it ends up leaving scars that last for the rest of our lives.

Falling in love with the wrong person can cut deeper than any other person on this earth hurting you. This is because we share a part of ourselves that no one else is getting. Our secrets, desires, goals as well as our bodies are being given to this individual and if it is not handled with care, it can crush us spiritually.

Contrary to popular belief, you cannot lay with someone and get up the same way you laid down. When you allow a man to enter you, you have agreed to take a part of him in exchange for a part of you. Those parts are forever with gone. Sex is just as spiritual as it is physical. This is why so many men and women are damaged today.

Once you have been promiscuous, you are now carrying all of the men that you have slept with. Be it a one night stand or a full out relationship. You become intertwined with each one of them. Depending on the length of time you have been sleeping with them you will start to notice a similarity coming over the two of you; for example, finishing each other's sentences or starting to look alike as some say. Do you really believe that is because of spending that much time together? No matter how long you have been with a person, you will never be able to read their mind. As for looking alike, well let's just say, you have taken in enough of their DNA to support minor changes. The point is the process of becoming One has begun at the onsite of sex. The original law was that once a man slept with a woman she became his wife because he has made a covenant with her.

    Many of us are not married yet because we have yet to be single, and the rest of us can't stay married because we have moved every Tom, Dick and Harry in with our husbands. There can only be one King at a time. So a Queen that walks into a domain with 7 Kings along with her, is going to make for a crowded house. Somebody is not going to make it.

So how do I cleanse myself from all these soul ties Makeda, you may ask? There is only one answer I can give, Detox. Whether your method is prayer, meditation or some other sort of ritual, it is your intention and declaration that will get the job done. You must break the cords, then clean up the residue. The residue is hurt or disappointment that came as a product of that union.

Agape Love

Agape Love is the greatest love of them all, it is selfless, sacrificial, unconditional love. It can be applied to anyone at any time. The problem is, most people do not know how to love selflessly. I would venture to say, most people do not know the beginning of understanding sacrificial love.

This particular Love Level is the Hardest to obtain but the most valuable to possess. At the point of knowing Agape Love, you then know the Creator. This is the type of love that He bestows on us, His Creation.

Empress Makeda Gordon

You have finally stopped looking for how love can serve you and started looking for how you can serve in love.

Agape in its essence is Complete Love. All types of love are within Agape but Agape does not lie within the other three. Learning to master the preceding three types of love is what prepares you for Agape.

This love requires infinite forgiveness and mercy. It is putting that person's needs before your own, making sure that you are considering them in every decision you make and most of all accepting them totally, flaws and all.

In order for one to feel safe enough to love someone on this level, you will have had to work out all of your issues, hurt and anything toxic in your life. Agape love can only come from the purest part of your being. It is a Godlike love. If you are unable to see God through this person, tread lightly. Be sure that your decision making and discernment is vibrating on a higher level.

Not every person will experience the opportunity to feel Agape for someone.

Therefore, if you find yourself there, be grateful and take pride because you have effectively cleansed and aligned your heart with your Creator.

ＥＭＰＲＥＳＳ ＭＡＫＥＤＡ ＧＯＲＤＯＮ

SELF EXPRESSION

Empress Makeda Gordon

Who Are You, and does anyone know? I am sure that is an odd question to ask in the minds of some, but it is relevant. When we think about Self Expression, we have to assume that one can only express what he or she is sure of. The truth is, that is not always the case. Some of us are who "they" say we are. That inspires another question; who are "they"? They, are the vast majority. The Media, Society, our Friend, Family, Bosses, and so on. I can be a daunting task to be clear on who we are when the influence on who we should be is go great. Is it possible that your Self Expression is really your Environmental Expression?

In this age of technology, we are bombarded with images of what a woman is, or what is acceptable as a woman. We are given subliminal messaging on the minute by minute basis. How to dress; what is proper speaking; the way we should walk; what our nails, hair and makeup should look like. How does one sift through all of this information to identify what she is versus what she has become? We have fads changing every couple of months, how does one keep up? Individuality is no longer what is "in". Not complying to celebrity fashion dos can lead to ridicule from other women. It can even determine your relationship status because a lot of men have bought into the propaganda.

Self-Expression: the process of making known one's thoughts or feelings or views

When we look at Self-Expression, we have to weigh if our external presence reflects our internal presence. If you do not see that as being true, it is time for us to find out why.

Starting with your moral fiber; what is your stance on how you interact with others, how to do view "right and wrong", what do you project to the world in terms of what you stand for? For example, let's just say that you stand for righteousness (whatever that means to you), are you able to say, in you day to day life that upon interaction with you, people around you are able to describe you in that manner? For instance, if you are a Muslima and that is the truth of who you are, because our faith weighs in heavily on our demeanor, do you present yourself as such? Is your head always covered, are you adorned with the proper garb at all times, does your speech depict that of what a true Muslima looks like? If any of your answers are No, you are not expressing yourself for yourself. That means if you are only presenting that person when you are around other women of the faith and become a chameleon with others, you are not being true to who you are. Therefore, your self-expression is not authentic, a woman that is sure of herself and stands by what she believes, is never altered or waivered by anyone.

    A woman that is Afrocentric will express that threw her attire. She may wear African garb, or wrap her head a certain way, she may also just wear colors that reflect an African flag from a country she is gravitated to; whatever the case when she walks down the street, there will be no question as to who she is and where her mind resides.

Another example of self-expression would be how well you are able to communicate your feelings. Some of us have a very hard time with speaking a firm YES or NO. We feel compelled to place others needs and feelings above our own, even when it is something that may be damaging to us. This particular behavior has been identified as the "people pleasing syndrome"; that is when a person has resigned to a lifestyle of taking care of others at all cost.

Most people who adopt this habit struggle with self-esteem issues. They don't view themselves as important, which causes them to do everything that is required of them in an effort to "keep the peace". A people pleaser is afraid of losing the ones they care about most. They are afraid of rejection and disapproval so they never speak up for themselves. In which case, they follow the majority versus standing in their own truth.

If you hear yourself in these words, you may have some unresolved issues that are muzzling your voice. It is as if the words are there that you want to say, but nothing comes out. After years of silence, it becomes frustrating; we become angry, which can escalate into bitterness. Once bitterness has set in, we lash in, yes, I meant to say "lash in". However, everyone in our path can feel the implosion about to happen.

When a person "lashes in", they begin to process a self-inflicted feeling of people always taking advantage of them. The negative self-talk is where the bitterness comes from. You have convinced yourself that how you are feeling, or, how people misuse and abuse you, is a reflection of them being selfish. Now, you are not entirely wrong about that. But, you have to look at it from a different perspective. For example, if you were offered housekeeping and chef services indefinitely for free, would you turn it down? Of course not. Who would? That, in essence, is how people view you, as the free help, and they maximize on it.

That challenge with it is not that they see you that way. The challenge is that you trained them to. The moment all of your vocabulary is reduced to one single word "Yes", You, not them, begun a trend of appropriate behavior. There lies the problem.

I do agree that some people do take advantage of kind hearted people just because they can. But, there is a difference between being kind hearted and being a doormat. Which are you?

Kind Hearted

Kind Hearted people will do whatever is within their power to help or support someone, anyone, that they feel deserves it. At times, they will go out of their way to be of help to someone in need. But, they do not sacrifice themselves or their families as a rule to do so.

Doormat

Doormats will do whatever it takes to help or support someone whether they feel they deserve it or not. They impose upon themselves all the time. They don't usually weigh the wants from the needs of the person asking. This type of person doesn't ask many questions they just act. They mentally and emotionally drain their own energy to ensure the other person's comfort. They are always the sacrificial lamb.

The common ground between the two is that they both have their hearts in the right place. The major difference between the two is that the Kind hearted person is comfortable saying No if need be, and the Doormat is not.

Once we identify which characteristic we are operating in, if it is the Doormat, we can search back to the point we made the decision to behave this way. In some cases, in may have been a child that was always craving attention to no avail; in other cases, it could have been the result of a controlling relationship. Controlling relationships tend to strip us of our voice and self-worth. It is our view of ourselves that give us the strength to speak up for ourselves.

Word gives Sound and Sound gives Power. When you state your stance on a topic and it is heard by whomever you are speaking to, it empowers you. It feels good to have your own set of morals and values; but it feels better to be able to be true to them.

One can learn so much through communication. As we communicate with someone, we not only are given the opportunity to teach, but we are also given the opportunity to learn. No one person has all the answers to all things. The one who believes so, is a foolish man. That is why it is so very important that we are guarding our minds from toxic information by choosing the company we keep carefully.

When the Good Book speaks about being "Equally Yoked", that is applicable to all areas of our lives; not just marriage. As we discussed earlier, the only group of people we do not choose is our families. However, we do get to sift through them and choose which ones we bring into our Inner Court.

Blood may very well be thicker than water, but, our bodies are made up of 60% water and 7% blood; I don't believe that those numbers have no significance. The only difference I see is that it would take longer to die from dehydration than it would bleeding out. Either way, they both can cause your death. Which means, you must maintain both to stay alive. My point here is, the world outside of your family is much larger, and you need outside connections as much as inside in order to survive in it. The wisdom comes in knowing the purity of either solution you are running through your body. Both can be infectious or toxic to you, so be mindful when replenishing.

There will be some hard decisions to make, if change is the goal, but necessary ones. The first is to take responsibility for your own actions and choices. As an adult, no one can force you to do anything that you do not want to do or are not comfortable with. You are the one that decided to please everyone else but yourself; but, you do not have to maintain that decision; Next, you have to put away the anger and bitterness that you have allowed to creep in based on your own decisions; Then you have to begin the process of re-training everyone you know.

When it comes to re-training, it is not as difficult as you may think. All it takes is a consistency of behaviors. When that one person that you have been enabling, comes to you again for money, weigh the need over the request; see to it that helping will not send your home into lack; then answer with a defined YES or NO. As you use this method of response repeatedly with that person, they will begin to see that it isn't so easy anymore and you will stop hearing those request as much, if at all. A mutual respect is gained; unless they are a User, in which case, they will probably slow down with dealing with you, as they are setting up their next enabler. Either way, you have regained your power from that individual. Repeat these steps with everyone you feel has taken advantage of you and watch out for new comers. Before you know it, you will see the quality of your life has improved. This technique works for managing your time as well.

So, Remember to SPEAK UP FOR YOURSELF; you are worth the peace of mind it gives.

WORD~SOUND~POWER

Empress Makeda Gordon

Honoring Your Intuition

Empress Makeda Gordon

In a world of technology, we have lost contact with the little voice within. Instead of using our hearts and minds to search out a concern, we simply look to the web for the answers. We have also adopted the habit of taking other people's opinions as truth. At what point do we tap into our God given ability to think for ourselves?

If we can remember back to being a child, you will see how our mode of operation was set on our gut feelings. If we didn't have a good feeling about something we didn't do it, or we did it knowing that there would be a repercussion, but somehow, we have disconnected from ourselves and connected to society's way of thinking and handling things. It's time we get back to the basics.

Empress Makeda Gordon

Intuition: the ability to understand something immediately, without the need for conscious reasoning.

Your ability to use your intuition is based on how in tuned you are with yourself. We all have that "little voice" in our heads that attempts to guide us throughout our lives. The problem is that we don't listen to it anymore; in some cases, we don't even know what the voice sounds like. It is in our best interest to become in tuned with ourselves.

Tuning: to adjust to the correct uniform pitch.

Operating through your intuitive senses takes some fine tuning. You will need to learn how to quiet the voices around you to hear the voice within you. That is not possible if you have a go to source in this natural realm. Do you believe that when we were created, everything that we needed was placed inside of you? If your answer was Yes, that is the beginning of this process.

The number one reason we look to others to talk to and advise us during hard times is a lack of trust in our own judgement. Every preceeding chapter that you have read up to this point has brought us to Intuitive perception. Intuitive perception comes when you are Grounded, Happy, Valuable, Loving Completely and able to be Self-Expressive. If any of these areas are out of alignment, you will have trouble clearly hearing your intuitive voice.

 Intuition goes past the hearing on a different level, it is also seeing from a different perspective. You hear and see things as they really are, not as you would like them to be. There is no filtering of information for you. It takes some practice, but it is an ability we all possess; yet few achieve. It truly is a meditative state of mind. A place of peace and serenity; very few things bother you there because every part of you understands that "it has to happen". It being whatever comes up in your life.

 See, when you have elevated yourself to a place of higher living; come into the understanding that The Most High makes no mistakes; start to make better decisions for your life, and surround yourself with good people, you have to know that if any trial emerges in your life, It Has To Happen. The

Most High only allows us to go through the hardships that we face for two reasons; He is trying to give us something that we have to be prepared to receive, or, He is trying to get something out of us that is not pleasing to Him and/or is harmful to you. Both scenarios cause us to grow.

If you have read Layers Vol. 1, you have learned how everything and everyone in our lives have a part in molding who we are as adults. However, working the exercises in Layers Vol. 1, should have allowed you to own all of the good and regurgitate all of the bad habits and thought processes. Not every woman has had an opportunity to get that type of help; which means that there are a lot of little Girls out here posing as Women and living through their Pain Bodies. Unless you have had the pleasure of walking through each of your friends lives and watching who they became as well as seeing the shedding of their lower selves, you can't really say that you are not taking advice from a pain driven little girl/boy. So, if that is not the case for you and your "advisees", you may want to start trusting your own intuition a bit more. At least you know your story.

There are many people that will criticize you for your way of thinking once your perception has changed or you've stopped telling them all of your business; it is up to you to get comfortable with that. Every pot sits on its own bottom; turning on a flame under my pot will not burn my friend, only me. So, in my opinion, if I am the one who has to deal with the heat, I'd rather be in control of the temperature.

When we start to talk about the visual aspect of intuition, everything is about perception versus reality and perception in reality. There is a difference between the two.

Perception vs Reality

Perception being one's interpretation and Reality being what is Real. An example of this would be an intoxicated person; now their perception is that there are two of you, but the reality is that there is only one. Why do you think that they can be so adamant about telling you that you have a twin present; it is because what they have taken into their system has altered their perception to a false reality. I bet you didn't know that it is very possible that you have been walking around intoxicated your entire life. If you don't believe me, let me show you something.

Have you ever met a female that you instantly clicked with? The two of you had so much in common; you began to do everything together all the time; your children played together and so on. Then one day, out of left field, she betrayed you in some way that broke your heart. Meanwhile, momma, sister, husband and everyone else that you introduced her to, kept warning you about her; never being able to put their finger on what it was, but there was something about her that rubbed everyone the wrong way, but you. Come to find out they were all right.

Now, keep in mind, It Had To Happen.

Once the friendship has ended, you start to look back, and what do you know; the signs were there the entire time. So with all of her red flags, how do you suppose you didn't see them? It was your perception of her versus her reality. Maybe you've never had many friends during your life; maybe you "just don't get along with women"; or perhaps you were at a place in your life that you needed a friend and she showed herself to be friendly. Whatever the reason, you chose to see her as you needed her to be, not as she was. This is a common mistake that we make when we are not using our intuition as a guide.

However, It Had To Happen. Why? People like this come into our lives for just a couple of reasons, but rarely for the ones they think; they are there to push you to the next level spiritually, IF, you are listening.

That woman's presence was there to teach you one of two possible lessons…

Lesson 1: To show you what you still have inside of you that needs to go. That's right, I said it. You only connected with such a person on that level and to the degree because something in her was able to communicate with something in you. So, that is a good place to conduct a character check on yourself.

Nothing happens by chance. It is from our spirits that we feel that instant gravitation to someone; that immediate connect. When you see that the person you connected to is a whole hot mess, nine times out of ten, you are too. You just may have learned how to mask it better and longer than most.

Lesson 2: You have no identity; you are still searching for yourself. A woman that is not in tune with herself does not know herself. They tend to be people who have friends of all types. Now, don't misunderstand me, I don't mean that our friendships should not be diversified. What I am saying is, a group of people that don't make any sense. Whether they are all at once or one after the other in terms of what point they are in your life.

For example, If you are a monogamous women who believes in loyalty, would you keep company with promiscuous women all the time? Of course not. Unless there is a part of you that is living through them or want to be like them. Just like if you are an extreme Spiritualist, you won't keep company with a bunch of religious people; again, unless you are interested in their way of life.

Having an identity crisis is not abnormal, we all go through that process, but the only way to resolve it is to look within. If you truly want to be your own person, that can't happen when you are being a chameleon. On the other hand, it is ok during your process to glean bits and pieces of other women and mold them into your own. Especially if you never had a woman in your life that you could look up to.

What I mean by that is this, if you have a friend that has been in a loving marriage for 10+ years, and you see how she cares for her husband, and admire that, it would be natural to say to yourself that you would like to be that type of wife. Because it is not the woman you are trying to become, it is only an attribute the woman possesses that you gravitate towards. Just be careful who you choose. Allow your intuition to guide you.

Perception in Reality

Self-alignment brings us to Perception IN Reality. That means that we see what is truly in front of us; we see through the mask that people wear. When you are tapped into your inner voice, it is not easy to pull the wool over your eyes. You will lose many friends and even some family once you have opened this place in you; but do not fear, those who walk away because they cannot walk over you, do not deserve to share your life with you.

Of course it appears to be easier to keep the rose colored glasses on, but does it really serve you? When we don't accept the truth about people, we end up being the ones to get hurt or betrayed by them. So, is it really easier to have to continue to lick your wounds because of your inability or refusal to be realistic?

I believe the late Maya Angelou said it best, "When people show you who they are, believe them". This statement changed my life. It is so simple, yet so profound, however, it seems to be the hardest thing to do. It is almost as if we opt for the pain and disappointment. The side effect of being in line with your intuition is that you are no longer able to put those glasses on.

Empress Makeda Gordon

We have now discussed six different layers of alignment. If one of these areas are out of place it will throw your entire balance off. Once that balance has been altered, your connection with The Most High is in jeopardy. It is in jeopardy because you will not be focused enough to seek Him, you will look to outside support versus leaning and depending on His guidance.

INTUITION

SELF-EXPRESSION

LOVING COMPLETELY

YOU ARE VALUABLE

HAPPINESS

GROUNDING

Each of these layers are connected and connect us to all creation.

Empress Makeda Gordon

WE ARE ONE

Empress Makeda Gordon

Connectedness is something we all look for as humans. We want to feel that we belong to something and someone outside of ourselves. Many of us spend our lives searching for connectedness in relationships, friendships, religions, etc.; once we obtain these things, somehow we still feel a void. Why is that? The reason is, you cannot fill a spiritual void with natural things.

Our quest starts very young as we begin to explore the world and the things around us. This is the reason that you will see children attaching themselves to stuffed animals, imaginary friends and such. The feeling of connection makes you feel secure. It is something about it that takes away the fear.

Bear with me for a moment, it is my belief that we are spiritual beings prior to taking on these natural shells of ours; spirits are complete and lacking nothing, but once we have be placed in these bodies we split into a triune being; now having a physical body, a soul and spirit. There is a different element or dimension that operates in each realm. The physical body does not exist until you are born, at which point our soul is breathed into us from the Most High; but the spirit is eternal. So we are forever searching for that level of completeness again. The only way to find that peace again, is to find the inner balance.

    This is why the prior layers we spoke about are so important to be aligned. That alignment is what opens up the portal to the spirit realm from which we came; and allows us to become One again. The opening gives us full access to the Creator and His creation.

    Where do we find this place of Oneness, or wholeness? We find it in all things. Every single thing that has been created is intertwined in some way. The answers we look for in our prayers and meditation lie within creation. That is why it is so important that we respect nature.

Empress Makeda Gordon

The information that you seek is not always written in a book. When you are spiritually connected you see the Creator in all things. You will be able to look at anything a find a lesson or an answer. For example, the ants, If you have ever watched a family of ants traveling to transport food to their nest, and see the value of team work. There is no way a single ant would be able to travel the distance and carry all that is needed to survive. They travel together and build together; but ants do not have the intellect that a human being has, so how is it that they have figured out this valuable lesson yet we can't? We still believe that we are an island to ourselves and instead of working together to survive we choose to struggle alone just to call ourselves independent.

The truth is, nothing and no one is truly independent. We all need each other, otherwise there would be no need for certain things to exist. That is what the circle of life.

The moment you are able to see God's presence in all things; you will have everything. The smarted man is a man with an open mind. A closed mind is unable to receive anything more than what it already possesses, but an open mind is capable of infinite wisdom. You must learn to empty your mind at times and just sit in a quiet space outside and watch; take a good long look around you and you will begin to see how you are completely cared for. If you just observe the operation of any species, you will notice that they have no worries, they move in confidence and are well kept. It is only humanity that carries so much stress. That stress we feel comes from overthinking everything.

Every living being knows exactly what to do to survive. It is an innate ability given to us all. The only difference is the brain power we possess. We have become so well educated that we no longer understand simplicity. Our Creator wants to pour out into our lives daily but that is not possible without the alignment process. There will be areas of your life that He can never penetrate because of the blockage we are causing through our toxic behaviors.

When we look at the picture a few pages back with the alignment diagram, you will see how much easier that out pouring will be. However, if we have shifts in those layers, we will experience a flow like a water hose with a crinkle in it; the water is flowing but it is either blocked completely or trickling out slowly.

All things flow from the top to bottom. Can you see how you not having balance can block your ability to receive all that you deserve? The beauty in it all is that we have not lost anything. Although you may not have had balance in your life all this time, your blessings are just stuck inside of you on one of your layers. Once you straighten yourself out you will see the flow break. All of the things that have been held up in your life, or, that you thought were denied, could very well be right there waiting on you.

Can you see it; can you see where you may be off track and need to re-align? Which area(s) do you feel is out of balance for you? Take some time to meditate on those areas and to bring them back into agreement with your Higher Self; your Spirit.

It helps to stay focused during meditation if you use color memory. I deliberately color coded each layer for you to make the balancing process easier. To pray is to talk, to meditate is to listen. It is time that we start listening to Him more than we are talking to Him. He has the answers. To guide you in a silent meditation, you can focus on the color of the emotion versus the emotion itself. That will keep you from wanting to complain during meditation.

Keep in mind that emotions are energy. They can either be positive or negative, but either way they are providing your body with the energy force you feed it. Balance the Energy and you balance your life.

Empress Makeda Gordon

Focus on your breathing; as you inhale, draw in positivity and as you exhale release the negative. Positivity is light and from God, negativity is darkness and from your adversary. So breath in light and breath out darkness.

If you find that the pain runs too deep for you to manage, you may want to seek some outside support.

May God bless you in your every effort.

Blessings Queens!

Epilogue

I cannot begin to thank you enough for allowing me to be a part of your journey. My earnest prayer for you, is to live a full and Balanced life, filled with love and prosperity.

A balanced life is a happy life. That doesn't mean that you will not have your challenges, we all do. The difference is how you will manage them from this point on.

Never settle for anything less than what the Queen deserves. There is no one that can dictate to you your worth. You have the right to take control of your life and make choices that serve You well. After all, it is only you that has to live with those choices.

I truly hope that you have had a chance to read Layers Vol. 1 by now; that is the foundational work that needs to be done in order to move forward with balancing out your life, a step 1 if you will. Volume 1 will help you to cut away the pain that has caused your imbalance to begin with.

Not addressing your pain body, It will stop you in your tracks and hinder your progress. . Your pain body will NOT allow you to grow; she needs you to stay subject to her; remember she is a scared little girl that is going to hold on for dear life. You must first give her rest, in order to move forward.

However, if you are reading this book first, you can still go back and do the ground work. You'll find applying this information, will be a lot easier, once the foundation is laid.

We will be closing out this series with Layers Volume 3 "Empress Order"; in that Vol. 3 we will dive into the deep. Our major focus will be breaking down what it means to live on a higher level and how to support the woman around you to do the same.

A major part of the healing process is to share and elevate your sisters. It is our duty to build each other; even in a world that wants us to tear each other down. We have to get back to building sisterhoods in your communities. I hope you are the Sphere Head in yours.

May Jah Rastafari Bless You Sister.

EMPRESS MAKEDA GORDON

Available Now

Make sure you get the Entire LAYERS Series….

Empress Makeda Gordon
Certified Holistic Healing Coach

Heights of Spirituality

Teachings of Rastafari

 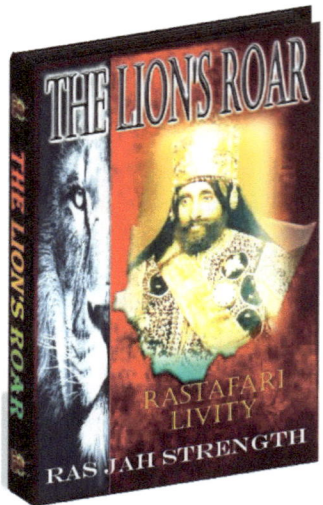

And for the Babies....
My African Me

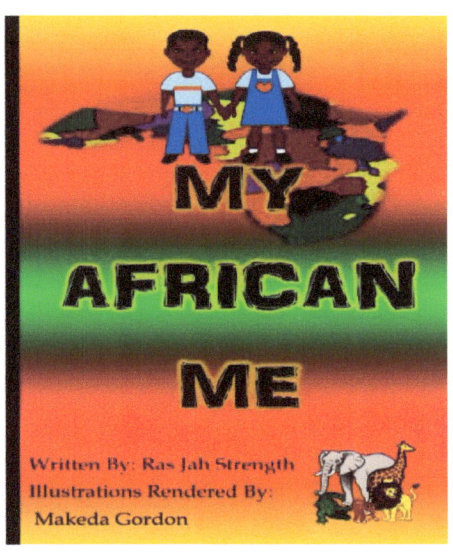

For more about Solomon & Makeda Publishing, or to make a purchase, visit us at www.sm4publishing.com

To Schedule an Empress Order Seminar/Sessions:

www.empressorder.com

Social Media:

Facebook @smpublishing

Instagram @s_mpublishing

Twitter @sm_publishing

Peace and Blessings!

www.ingramcontent.com/pod-product-compliance
Lightning Source LLC
Chambersburg PA
CBHW040355190426
43201CB00037B/10